Harriet Tubman

The Path to Freedom

By Diane DeFord

HAMERAY
PUBLISHING GROUP

Published in the United States of America
by the Hameray Publishing Group, Inc.

Text © Diane DeFord
Maps © Hameray Publishing Group, Inc.
Published 2009

Publisher: Raymond Yuen
Series Editors: Adria F. Klein and Alan Trussell-Cullen
Project Editor: Kaitlyn Nichols
Designers: Lois Stanfield and Linda Lockowitz
Map Designer: Barry Age

Photo Credits: AP: pages 19, 23
Corbis: front cover and pages 1, 4, 18
Getty: back cover and pages 12–13, 25, 29, 33

ISBN 978-1-60559-061-5

Printed in China

1 2 3 4 5 SIP 13 12 11 10 09

Chapter 3

A Blow to the Head

For many years Edward Brodess hired Minty out to work at nearby farms. She plowed the fields, drove the ox, and hauled logs. She became very strong.

> *Slave owners sometimes hired out their slaves to do jobs for other people. The slave owners would then get paid for the work their slaves did.*

But Minty liked staying at home best. She loved to look after her little brothers and sisters. But then Edward Brodess sold her three older sisters and sent them away.

Then another slave owner wanted to buy her little brother, Moses. Minty helped her mama hide him. They hid him for a month. But then Edward Brodess came to the

cabin with the other slave owner to get Moses.
Minty watched her mother stand up to them.

▼ A group of slaves
working on a plantation.

She yelled at the owner. "You are after my son," she said. "The first man that comes into my house, I will split his head open!"

The men looked at Minty's mama for a moment. Then they turned and left. Minty saw that when her mama stood firm it stopped them.

But one day, when Minty was twelve, everything changed. She went to the store to buy supplies. Then she heard shouting. She ran outside. She saw a slave run by. The slave ran from a white man with a whip. The man shouted at Minty to stop the slave but Minty yelled back, "No!"

The man saw an iron weight. He picked it up and threw it at the slave. It missed the slave but hit Minty on the head. In her words, "It broke my skull." She fell to the ground with her head bleeding and did not move. She was never the same again.

Chapter 4

A New Name, a New Life

Minty had headaches, dreams, and visions after that. She also fell asleep a lot. Sometimes she fell down, too. People thought she wasn't smart anymore.

Edward Brodess tried to sell her, but no one wanted to buy her. He still hired her out to do heavy work. But she also had many days when she was too sick to work.

In 1844 Minty married a free African-American. His name was John Tubman. She took her husband's last name. She took a new first name, too. She used her mama's name, Harriet. She was no longer Minty. Now she was Harriet Tubman. But she was still a slave.

Her early life had made Harriet a fighter. She had watched her mama fight to keep her family. She had watched her father fight to keep them alive. Harriet learned that to be free, she must also fight. The call to be free became stronger every day.

> "I had reasoned this out in my mind, there was one of two things I had a right to, liberty or death; if I could not have one, I would have the other."
>
> —Harriet Tubman

Chapter 5

Escape from Captivity

When Edward Brodess died in 1849, his wife Eliza had to sell his slaves. Harriet was afraid her family would be split up and sold. She wanted to act first. Her husband did not agree. But in September, she and her two brothers, Ben and Harry, went to work on a **plantation**. This was their chance to escape. On the 17th they ran away.

It was two weeks before Eliza Brodess knew they were gone. She offered a reward to get them back. Ben and Harry were afraid. They wanted to go back home. They made Harriet go home, too.

▲ A poster offering a reward for the capture of a runaway slave.

Soon Harriet tried to escape again. This time, she went alone. Before she left, she sang a song to another slave. It was a message meant for her mama. "I'll meet you in the morning, I'm bound for the Promised Land."

Harriet ran north. She had no money, no friends, and only the North Star to lead the way. She had two names on a piece of paper. They were the names of people who would provide places to hide—her first safe houses on the Underground Railroad.

▲ A historic marker of the Underground Railroad.

At her first stop, a woman had her sweep the front yard. It made her look like she worked for them. That night, she hid in a cart and she rode to the next safe house.

She went on, walking by night and sleeping by day. The men and women of the Underground Railroad helped.

She walked ninety miles to reach her goal of freedom. Harriet had made it to Philadelphia, Pennsylvania, where she could be free.

In Philadelphia, she cleaned houses and saved money. But she missed her family. Her love of family led her to the next part of her life's journey.

> *"I had crossed the line. I was free; but there was no one to welcome me to the land of freedom. I was a stranger in a strange land."* —**Harriet Tubman**

Chapter 6

The Slave Sale

Harriet thought about her family all the time. She was free but she was alone. And her family members were still slaves. They were too afraid to do what Harriet had done. She had to go back for them. She worked and saved. And she prayed.

But in 1850 a new law was passed. Its name was the **Fugitive Slave Law**. It said police would help capture runaway slaves. The police would capture them even in free states in the North. They had to arrest people who hid slaves, too.

Then, in December of 1850, Harriet got a message. There was a slave sale.

Eliza Brodess wanted to sell Harriet's niece and her two babies. Harriet had to help. She went to Baltimore, Maryland and hid at Tom Tubman's house. He was her husband's brother. She made a plan.

Her niece's husband was a free man. On the day of the sale, he made a bid for his wife. His bid won. While he went to pay, his wife ran with the two children. They ran to a safe house.

That night, they rode up the river in a log canoe. Harriet went to meet them. She took them to Philadelphia. Part of her family was free. But there were many more trips on the Underground Railroad ahead of her.

A poster warning ▶
of slave catchers.

CAUTION!!

COLORED PEOPLE

OF BOSTON, ONE & ALL,

You are hereby respectfully CAUTIONED and advised, to avoid conversing with the

Watchmen and Police Officers of Boston,

For since the recent ORDER OF THE MAYOR & ALDERMEN, they are empowered to act as

KIDNAPPERS

AND

Slave Catchers,

And they have already been actually employed in KIDNAPPING, CATCHING, AND KEEPING SLAVES. Therefore, if you value your LIBERTY, and the *Welfare of the Fugitives* among you, *Shun* them in every possible manner, as so many *HOUNDS* on the track of the most unfortunate of your race.

Keep a Sharp Look Out for KIDNAPPERS, and have TOP EYE open.

APRIL 24, 1851.

Chapter 7

The Conductor

Harriet went back to Maryland again and again. She was a "**conductor**" for the Underground Railroad. She brought back her family. She brought back other people, too. She took them to Canada. With each trip she grew more confident.

Harriet Tubman Wanted!

Helping slaves escape could get Harriet in a lot of trouble. By 1856, there was a $40,000 reward for her capture. That was a lot of money back then.

She learned a lot of tricks, too. One time, she wore a bonnet and carried two live chickens. When she saw a slave owner from her home, she pulled the chickens' legs. They made a lot of noise and she got away.

▲ Harriet Tubman (far left) with a group of escaped slaves.

Another time, she was on a train and she saw a man she knew. She put a newspaper in front of her face and pretended to read. Everyone knew Harriet couldn't read so he didn't think it was her. Amazingly, she got away yet again.

Harriet Tubman carried a gun to fight against **slave catchers** and protect her "**passengers**." She never lost a single one of them. Word of her success spread. She made at least nineteen trips by 1860. People called her "Moses" because, like Moses, she led her people to freedom.

> *"I was a conductor of the Underground Railroad for eight years, and I can say what most conductors can't say: I never ran my train off the track and I never lost a passenger."*
> —Harriet Tubman

Chapter 8

Nurse and Union Spy

In 1861 the Civil War began. Harriet wanted to help in the war. If the North won, she thought it would end slavery. So she joined the Union army. She went to South Carolina.

The Civil War

There were two sides in the Civil War: One side was the Union, *which was the U.S. Federal Government and the free states in the North. On the other side was* the Confederacy, *which was the eleven slave states in the South. The Confederacy decided that they wanted to form their own country and seceded from the U.S.*

At first, Harriet was a nurse. She also helped slaves escape. She helped them find work. Then she went to Florida. She nursed the sick and wounded soldiers. She even made medicine from roots and plants. To earn money, she baked and sold pies and homemade root beer.

Harriet wanted freedom for all her people. Then she met Union General David Hunter. He set all the slaves free that he found. He even made a unit of African-American soldiers.

Then in 1863 President Abraham Lincoln wrote the Emancipation Proclamation.

The Emancipation Proclamation

To emancipate means to set free. A proclamation is an official announcement. Lincoln's Emancipation Proclamation said that all slaves living in the South would be freed if the slave states did not rejoin the Union by January 1, 1863.

▲ Abraham Lincoln was the sixteenth president
of the United States.

This was the first step that led to freedom for slaves.

In 1863 Harriet became a Union spy. She was good at this, too. She led parties of scouts behind enemy lines. She met key people and told them what she heard and saw. She even led armed men in battle.

Harriet lived to see slavery **abolished** in 1865. The war had ended and the **Thirteenth Amendment** to the Constitution had made slavery illegal in every state. This was what Harriet Tubman had fought for and now the right to freedom had been won.

Chapter 9

Fighting for the Right to Vote

There was one more battle to fight. Women could not vote. And Harriet's life showed that she was equal to men. So she went to speak in New York City, Boston, and Washington, D.C.

Harriet told her own story. She told people what she did to free slaves. She told people what she did during the war. She told about other women in history who were brave and equal to men. She said women had earned the right to vote.

Ten years later, women won the right to vote. Harriet did not live long enough to get to vote. But she was a brave fighter in this war, too.

The Nineteenth Amendment

The Nineteenth Amendment was a change to the U.S. Constitution made on August 26, 1920. It changed the laws of the country to say that denying someone the right to vote because of their sex was illegal.

As Harriet grew old, her head injury hurt even more. She found a doctor who preformed surgery. It made her last ten years easier. But by 1911, she was very frail. She went to stay in a rest home named after her.

Harriet Tubman died on March 10, 1913. She was ninety-three years old. During her life, people respected her. After her death, people **revered** her.

Timeline

About 1820   Araminta Ross (later known as Harriet Tubman) is born in Maryland

1832   Is hit on the head; the injury affects her for the rest of her life

1844   Marries John Tubman and changes her name to Harriet

1849   Escapes to Philadelphia; begins to work on the Underground Railroad

1850   The Fugitive Slave Law is passed; Tubman frees her niece

1850– 1860   Made nineteen trips to free slaves and take them to Canada

1861   Civil War begins, April

1861– Worked as a nurse and a spy for
1865 the Union Army in the Civil War;
helps slaves find jobs

1863 President Lincoln issues the
Emancipation Proclamation

1865 Civil War ends, April

1865 Thirteenth Amendment is passed,
making slavery illegal in the U.S.,
December 6

1913 Dies on March 10, 1913, in the nursing
home named after her

1920 The Nineteenth Amendment is passed,
giving women the right to vote,
August 26

Glossary

abolished ended the practice of something

conductor a train driver, used as a name for those who helped guide slaves to freedom on the Underground Railroad

Fugitive Slave Law a law passed in 1850 that forced the police to arrest escaped slaves or anyone who helped slaves run away

passengers a traveler; used as a name for slaves who were taken to safety by a guide

plantation a large farm or estate on which crops such as cotton, coffee, or tobacco are planted

revered	to appreciate greatly
scouts	people who go ahead to explore an area or to find out information about an enemy
slave catchers	people who caught escaped slaves
Thirteenth Amendment	an addition to the U.S. Constitution made in 1865. It made slavery illegal in every state in America.
Underground Railroad	a network of safe houses that made up an escape route for slaves
Union spy	a person who collected information about the Confederates and gave it to the Union soldiers

Learn More

Books

Harriet Tubman: A Woman of Courage (Time for Kids) by Time for Kids Editors (HarperCollins, 2005)

Moses: When Harriet Tubman Led her People to Freedom by Carole Boston Weatherford (Hyperion, 2006)

The Story of Harriet Tubman: Conductor of the Underground Railroad by Kate McMullen (Yearling, 1990)

Wanted Dead or Alive: The True Story of Harriet Tubman by Ann McGovern (Scholastic, 1991)

Websites

www.harriettubman.com

www.nyhistory.com/harriettubman/life.htm

www.pbs.org/wgbh/aia/part4/4p1535.html

www2.lhric.org/POCANTICO/tubman/tubman.html

Index